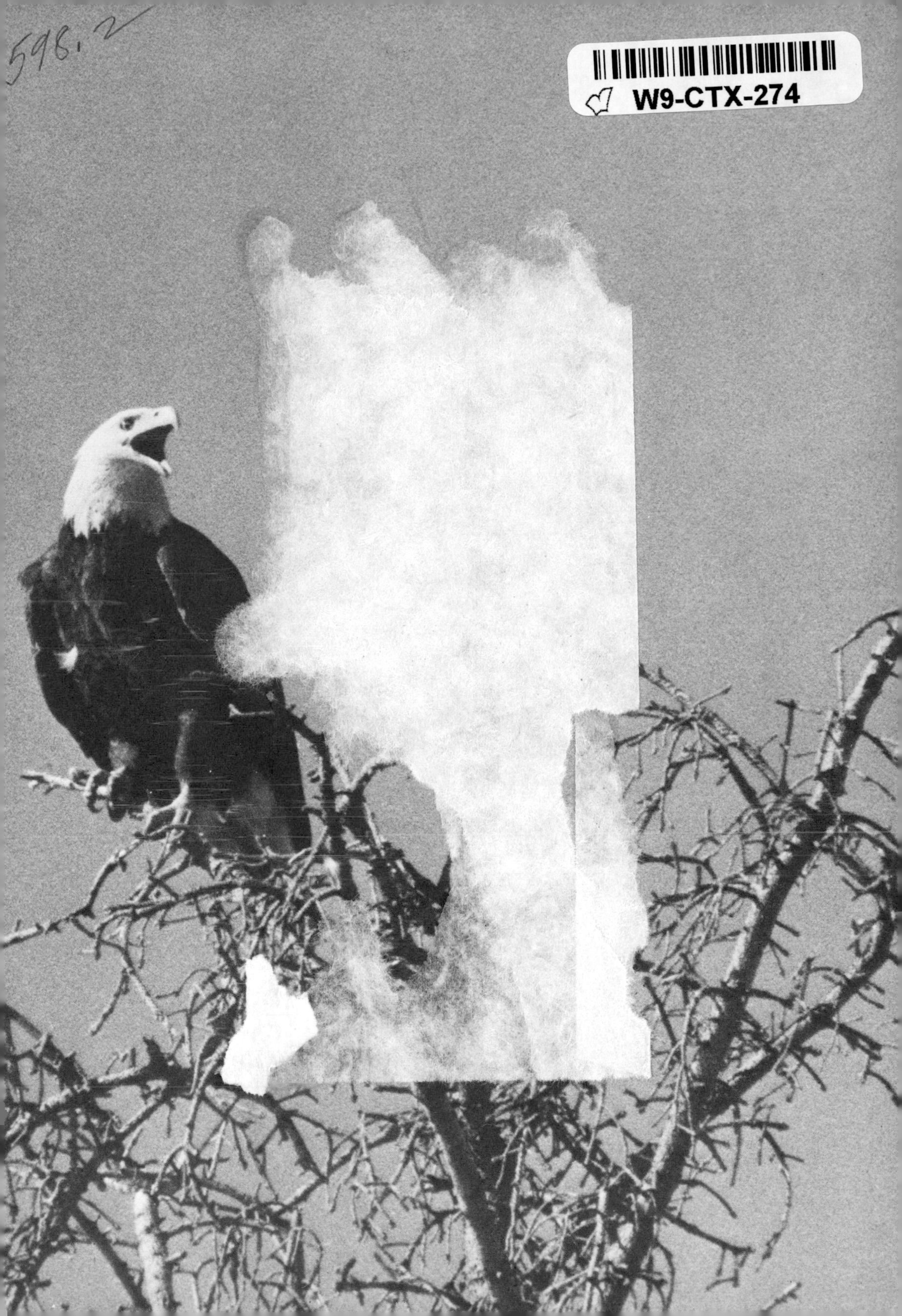

The Magnificent Bald Eagle

Here, in words and photographs, is a
vivid closeup portrait of a Bald Eagle
family in the rugged Teton Mountains
of Wyoming.

The book follows an eagle family
through courtship, nesting, and the
hatching of the young bird, Tally.

The eagle parents protect and feed
Tally. Later they teach him how to be
a skillful flyer and an expert hunter,
living in harmony with the other animals
of the mountain wilderness.

But the wilderness is threatened,
and so is Tally's future. The last chapter
of this book suggests what we must do
if we wish to save America's national bird.

The Magnificent Bald Eagle

America's National Bird

by John F. Turner

photographs by the author

RANDOM HOUSE NEW YORK

This title was originally catalogued by the Library of Congress as follows:

Turner, John F
    The magnificent bald eagle, America's national bird, by
John F. Turner. Photos. by the author. New York, Random House ₁1971₎

    81 p. illus. 24 cm.

    SUMMARY: Discusses the danger to the bald eagle from hunters,
pollution, and pesticides by following the activities of an eagle
family.

    1. Bald eagle—Juvenile literature. ₁1. Bald eagle. 2. Eagles₎
I. Title.

PZ10.T87Mag   598.9′1   73–158383
ISBN 0–394–92061–9   MARC

Library of Congress   71 ₁4₎   A C

Trade Ed.: ISBN: 0-394-82061-4   Lib. Ed.: ISBN: 0-394-92061-9

*For helpful suggestions in the preparation
of this book, the author and the publisher are
grateful to Dr. Sergej Postupalsky, Department of
Wildlife Ecology, University of Wisconsin.*

PHOTOGRAPH CREDITS:
*John F. Turner provided all the photographs in
this book except on the following pages:
Page 6 (from the Museum of the City of New York);
pages 9 and 73 (from United Press International).*

Designed by Herb Levitt

Contents

The Magnificent Bald Eagle

America's Bald Eagle

A few hundred years ago America was fresh and beautiful. Tall green forests and lush prairies covered most of the land. Everywhere the water and the air were clean. Everywhere America was full of animals.

Throughout the vast wild land lived a magnificent white-headed eagle. Thousands of these great birds built their huge nests and raised their families along the shores of oceans, lakes, and rivers.

This bird became known as the American Bald Eagle. But the eagle is not really bald. His head and neck are covered with pure white feathers. His tail is also white, while the feathers of the body and wings are dark brown. His beak, his feet, and his eyes are a bright yellow.

Weighing ten to thirteen pounds, the Bald Eagle is the largest hunting bird on the North American continent. His body is about three feet long. But when he spreads his wings, they measure six to eight feet across.

The first human beings to live in our land were the American Indians. They admired the eagles and lived in harmony with them. For the Indians the eagles were sacred birds, to be honored for their beauty, strength, and courage.

The eagle was known to some Indians as "Thunderbird." They believed that thunder came from the flapping of his great wings.

The Indians were fine storytellers, and many of their tales were about eagles. One Indian legend said that the Bald Eagle was the only bird able to fly to the sun and to push it across the sky. According to the legend, the sun's great heat turned the eagle's head and tail feathers white.

The eagle was important to many
Indian tribes in other ways. Once a
warrior proved himself in battle, he was
permitted to wear eagle feathers in his
hair. The feathers were a sign of the
Indian's strength and bravery. He used
them to decorate his war shields and
clothing. He fitted small eagle feathers
into the ends of arrows to make them
fly straight.

The Bald Eagle was especially important to the Iroquois Indians in the eastern part of our country. The symbol for their government was a pine tree which they regarded as a source of life. Over the tree they placed the Bald Eagle as a symbol of protection and strength.

When European settlers came to America, they were already familiar with eagles. Although only the Bald Eagle and the Golden Eagle live in North America, there are more than fifty kinds of eagles on other continents. People in many parts of the world have admired eagles for thousands of years.

The New York seal includes a settler, an Indian, and a Bald Eagle.

The eagle was an important symbol in the ancient empires of Egypt and Greece. Later, for Rome's mighty armies, the eagle was a sign of victory and power.

In the United States, the Bald Eagle is the main figure of our national seal. The history of our Great Seal is almost as old as the history of our country.

Our Declaration of Independence was accepted by the Second Continental Congress on July 4, 1776. That same day Congress decided the brand-new nation should have its own seal. All other countries had seals, but most of them used the coats of arms of ruling families. America had no ruling families. It was a new kind of country with new freedoms, new hopes, and a new democratic way of life. America was a special country and needed a special seal.

It took six years of discussion before the Congressmen could agree on a design for the new seal. Finally they chose the Bald Eagle for the central figure, because the eagle seemed a good symbol for the bold, free spirit of the new country. And since the Bald Eagle lives only in North America, he is truly an American bird. On the seal the eagle holds the olive branch of peace in one foot and the arrows of strength in the other.

The picture of our national bird
appears often in our everyday life. We
find the American eagle on coins, seals,
dollar bills, government buildings, sport
uniforms, advertisements, and even
on buttons. The Bald Eagle has been
pictured more times than any other
animal in the world.

Yet few Americans today have ever
seen a Bald Eagle in real life. Sights of
this wild, beautiful creature are becoming
rarer and rarer.

Today some Bald Eagles make their
homes in the wilderness regions of Alaska
and Canada. There are eagles still
living in remote areas of Florida, Maine,
Michigan, Minnesota, and Wisconsin.
A few more live in undisturbed places
scattered across America.

One of these places is a beautiful
valley tucked high in the Teton Mountains of Wyoming. This place is called
Eagle Valley.

Eagle Valley

Eagle Valley is a long, hidden pocket of land surrounded by snow-capped peaks. Small streams tumble from the rugged mountain slopes and canyons. The streams join a large river called Wild River, which winds through the length of the valley.

Now, in winter, heavy snows blanket the land. Ice covers the lakes and ponds. But the waters of Wild River are too restless to turn to ice.

Watching the river intently, a Bald Eagle is perched high in a leafless tree. The bird is an adult male. With his strong coloring of dark brown, bright yellow, and white, he makes a striking picture against the blue sky. He is waiting for a careless fish to swim up near the surface from the darker depths.

Suddenly the eagle drops from his perch. He opens his large wings and makes a rapid turn toward the icy water. With great speed his plunge brings him over the water's surface at a low angle.

His powerful feet strike beneath the surface. A cold spray splashes up under his belly and wings, but his body stays above the water. In an instant his strong wing beats carry him up and away.

He rises with a fish wiggling in his sharp claws, called "talons."

The eagle carries his catch to a gravel bar, where he lands and begins his meal. Holding the fish on the ground with his feet, he tears off pieces of flesh with his large curved beak. He lifts his head and quickly gulps down each piece.

The eagle's mate is fishing nearby. In coloring she is exactly like the male, but in size she is somewhat larger.

Winter can be a difficult time for wildlife. Many of the valley's animals are tucked safely in homes beneath the deep snow. High on the mountain slopes the Silvertip Grizzly Bears are sleeping in their winter dens.

A short distance upriver a Moose is wintering in a patch of willows. When he is hungry he nibbles the tender ends of the willow stems. Sometimes a Coyote will pass by in search of mice or perhaps a piece of food which the eagles have dropped.

Most of Eagle Valley's birds have flown south for the winter. But Bald Eagles are tough and hardy birds. Lord and Lady Eagle remain in this valley the entire year.

For the hunters food is scarce this
time of year. The lakes and ponds are
capped with ice. So the eagles spend long
hours hunting the open waters of Wild
River. They must eat more food in
winter because they need extra energy to
keep their bodies warm.

The eagle pair seldom visit their
nest in midwinter. They spend most of
their time far upriver where winter
fishing is best. They sleep in favorite
perches—branches of giant trees near the
river.

Lord and Lady Eagle have lived on
Wild River for many years. Long ago
they chose this section of the river for
their home. Partners for life, they will
live together here until one of them dies
—perhaps at the age of twenty to thirty
years.

When the eagle pair started nesting
here, the nest was already many years
old. Each year they have added sticks and
other building materials so that now
the nest is higher than a standing man.
And it is as wide as it is high.

The nest is set in the top branches
of an old Cottonwood tree, more than
a hundred feet above the ground.

It is late February in Eagle Valley. Cold slashing blizzards and sub-zero temperatures are still frequent visitors to Wild River. Yet Lord and Lady Eagle begin to visit the nest more often.

From time to time Lady Eagle lands on the nest to clear away the fluffy white snow. Soon she and her mate begin to repair their nest for the new season. They pick up some sticks from the ground where the snow is not deep. But they get most of their building material in a more daring fashion.

Lord Eagle chooses a dead branch in a nearby tree. Then he rises in the air until he is well above the limb. With a sudden plunge he dives with outspread legs. His talons are open to hit and then grab the branch. With a sharp crack his moving weight breaks it off. Sometimes such a branch is several feet long. He carries it to the nest.

Lady Eagle usually performs the task of weaving the new stick into place. She pads the center of the nest with softer materials such as grass, leaves, feathers, pieces of bark, or even clumps of soft earth. Except for a slight hollow in the middle, the surface of the big nest is quite flat.

On sunny days, Lord and Lady Eagle often glide high above Wild River. With outstretched wings they fly in large lazy circles, taking advantage of the warm air which rises near the river and drifts high into the sky. These air currents carry the gliding eagles upward. The birds soar higher and higher until they appear from the ground to be tiny dots in a great world of blue.

This is the time of year for the courtship of Lord and Lady Eagle. It begins one day when the two eagles are soaring in large circles high above the floor of the valley. They seem restless. As if playing, one of them often chases the other. They dip and turn in the sky. Sometimes one of them screams.

Suddenly the two come together and lock their feet. With their great wings partially tucked, they fall earthward. For hundreds of feet they rocket downward together—plunging and tumbling. As they near the ground, they suddenly separate. Opening their wings, they scream and swoop upward with the air currents. In the next few days they repeat this act many times.

At this time the male fertilizes an egg within the female. Once the egg is fertilized, a baby eagle begins to live and grow.

Throughout March, Lady Eagle spends more and more time on the nest platform. The time for egg laying finally comes.

She usually lays two eggs in late March. This year, however, she lays only one. The egg is chalky white and about twice as big as a chicken's egg.

Lady Eagle begins to incubate the egg immediately. She nestles over it with her warm body so that it is tucked snugly in her soft belly feathers.

The egg must be kept warm at all times. If it were left alone, the cold temperature would quickly freeze it.

During April, warmer days announce the arrival of a new season. Lady Eagle sits hour after hour warming the egg. From time to time she rises, bends over, and gently turns the egg with her beak.

With the approach of spring, Lady Eagle notices many busy changes coming to Eagle Valley. The towering Teton peaks are still white with winter snow. But on the valley floor, small streams of melting snow trickle from shrinking snow fields.

At first a few birds—and then more and more—return from the south. Many will stop in Eagle Valley for the nesting season. Others are heading farther north, using the river as a path to follow. Flying in V formation, the Canadian Geese pass overhead. With steady honking, they loudly announce their return to the hidden valley.

Lady Eagle sees a large brown animal walking awkwardly down the river bank. It is the old bull Buffalo which has spent the winter months far upriver on some wind-swept grass ridges. He wanders close to the nest tree, stops to drink from a pond of water, and then continues slowly downriver.

In the distance Lady Eagle sees her mate chase and catch a duck along the river. Lord Eagle carries it to a perch, holds it down with one foot, and then carefully plucks out the feathers with his beak. The plucking takes almost half an hour.

Carrying the plump duck in his talons, he flies back to the nest. Lady Eagle greets him and his catch with chirps. Lord Eagle glides down, folds his wings, and settles to the nest. He places the duck next to Lady Eagle and then flies to a nearby tree.

Lady Eagle turns her attention to the duck. She rips off chunks of meat and gulps them down. When she finishes eating, she chirps to her mate. Lord Eagle leaves his perch, flies to the nest, and settles gently down over the egg.

Lady Eagle picks up the duck bones and flies away from the nest. Out toward the willow patch she drops them to the ground.

Throughout April, Lord and Lady Eagle have taken turns incubating the egg. Five weeks have passed since Lady Eagle laid it. Then, one day, the eagle parents hear soft chirps inside the egg.

Tally

Shortly after Lady Eagle laid her egg, a tiny heart started to beat within. At first the baby eagle was very small. He rested near the middle of the egg on the ball of yellow yolk. A lighter-colored fluid surrounded the yolk.

Like all growing animals, this little eagle must have fresh air and food. Air reaches him through the eggshell. The fluids inside the egg are his food supply, which he absorbs into his body as he grows.

Within the egg he finally begins to
move his head, his legs, his wing limbs.
He twists his small body from side to
side. This exercise helps him gain the
muscle strength he will need to escape
from the shell.

As he grows, he takes up more and
more room inside the shell. Several weeks
pass and most of his food supply is
used up.

Now the little eagle, Tally, is growing restless. He squirms and wriggles
more often. He begins to chirp.

It is now early May in Eagle Valley.
The fullness of spring has finally come.
Most of the snow which blanketed
the valley floor through the long winter
has disappeared.

New green plants are sprouting in
the meadows. Great White Pelicans,
ducks, and many kinds of song birds are
still returning to Eagle Valley from the
south. More than two months have
gone by in Eagle Valley since Lord and
Lady Eagle first began their nesting
duties.

Early May is the time of hatching
for the baby eagle. Hatching from the
shell is hard work for a little bird—
even for an eagle. Like other baby birds,
however, Tally has an "egg tooth" to
help him break through the shell. The

23

egg tooth, which will disappear after
hatching, is a small horn-like bump on
top of his little beak.

One warm sunny morning Tally
knocks a couple of times against the shell.
He rests awhile, and then knocks again.
The baby eagle makes peeping sounds,
and his parents answer with soft chirps.

After several hours a thin crack
appears in the middle of the shell. As he
keeps on knocking, Tally very slowly
turns inside the shell. As he turns and
knocks, the crack grows longer around
the shell.

The long task requires a great
amount of energy for the little eagle. As
Tally becomes tired, he takes longer rest
periods. But each time he starts to
work again.

Finally a large portion of the shell
comes loose. With a great amount of
struggling, Tally rolls free of the shell.

The hatching has taken nearly all
day, and Tally lies exhausted in the
bottom of the nest. For the first time he
feels the warmth of the late afternoon
sun on his damp skin. Soon his tiny wet
feathers dry out. Now he is dressed
in a coat of light, soft, fluffy feathers
called "down." He is only a few inches
long and weighs about three ounces.

Lord Eagle removes the pieces
of shell from the nest. Lady Eagle gently
settles over Tally until he is snuggled
in her soft warm belly feathers. While
Tally is small and helpless, one of his
parents will watch over and care for him
constantly. Lady Eagle does most of
this brooding.

When the weather is chilly, Tally is
tucked safely under the warm body of
his mother. He must also be protected
from rain and from the sun's hot rays. To
do this one of his parents will crouch
over him with partly open wings. Tally
rests comfortably under this feather
umbrella for hours at a time.

Lord Eagle continues to hunt for
the family's food. Whenever he catches
a prey, he takes it in his talons and flies
back to the nest. Tally can eat several
meals a day. His body, growing rapidly,
needs a great deal of energy and building
materials.

Sometimes Tally spots the arrival
of food from far away. He greets his
father with loud chirps and moves restlessly about the nest as Lord Eagle
approaches.

When Tally is still small, he eats
with the help of one of his parents.
Usually his mother feeds him. She rips
apart the prey with her strong beak and
then gives small pieces to her son. Even
after being fed, he will sometimes peck
at his parents as if to ask for more.

Lord and Lady Eagle can catch and
eat a wide variety of animal food. But
their favorite food is fish. That is why,
like other Bald Eagles, they nest near
a body of water.

Wild River supplies Lord and Lady Eagle with fish throughout most of the year. During the spring, however, the waters of melting snows pour into the winding river. It then becomes high and muddy. For a few weeks the eagles find it difficult to fish in the murky water. During this time the parent eagles spend more effort hunting birds, such as ducks and Coots—sometimes even woodpeckers, geese, and herons. They also look for small mammals—ground squirrels, rabbits, Muskrats.

As the days of May slip by, Eagle Valley becomes greener. The days and nights become warmer. Most of the snow has melted from the lower mountain slopes.

The little eagle grows quickly. Three weeks after hatching, Tally begins to change in appearance. His first light-gray coat of down feathers is slowly replaced by a second coat of dark-gray down. This second feather covering is thicker and fuzzier.

Tally's weight is now already half that of an adult Bald Eagle. Some parts of his body have grown faster than others. His beak, his feet, and his talons are almost as large as an adult's.

Even now his talons are sharp and his feet can strike with lightning speed. With them, he could deliver severe blows to any intruder in the nest. His powerful feet will soon grip with almost as much strength as a man's hand.

With the coming of summer, many things are happening in Eagle Valley. Everywhere wild creatures, small and large, are busy at work and play. From his high home Tally sees many new things. His eyesight is very keen.

Far below, and out in a nearby meadow, he watches small butterflies move among the young plants. They light gently on the spring flowers, rest quietly, and then quickly flutter to new ones.

Looking toward the willow patch beside the river, he sees the eagle family's largest neighbor, the Moose. He is nibbling on fresh willow buds. Behind his ears are growing this year's new pair of paddle-shaped antlers.

Along the rolling sagebrush ridge Tally can see the movements of some large tan animals. These are small herds of Rocky Mountain Elk. Every spring they move back up through Eagle Valley from their wintering grounds to the south. They are on their way to their summer range in the mountains to the north.

Behind some of the large Elk follow little ones with wobbly legs. These are the Elk calves which have just been born this spring.

From the nest Tally can also see Beavers gliding through their pond with freshly cut willows in their teeth. The pond has backed up behind the dam built by the Beavers out of sticks and mud.

Not far from the Beavers' house, a pair of great white Trumpeter Swans are making a nest in the same pond. The swans, each weighing about twenty-five pounds, feed on plants from below the water's surface.

The swans do not compete with the eagles for animal food. Lord and Lady Eagle will not disturb them. However, the eagle pair have established a "nesting territory" around their nest tree. This is an area which the eagle parents will protect from intruders.

They will defend their territory
against certain hawks, falcons, and other
eagles—hunting birds which would
compete with them for the limited supply
of animal food. The nesting territory
also protects young Tally from hunting
birds which might harm him.

When trespassers do wander into
the nesting territory, Lord and Lady
Eagle give warnings with their chirping
screams. If the warnings go unheeded,
one of the eagles will fly at the intruder.
Defending their nesting territory against
another hunting bird, either of the
eagle parents is a deadly force. No
trespassing bird will dare stay to fight.

One day Tally suddenly hears
screams from both of his parents. The
noise startles him. He looks out to where
Lord and Lady Eagle are circling.
Below them on Wild River floats a long
narrow object. Within it are two strange
animals. Lord and Lady Eagle swoop
down near the floating animals and
continue their screams.

Tally has never seen his parents
behave like this before. He crouches low
in the nest. He does not know who these
unwanted visitors on Wild River are.

But Lord and Lady Eagle recognize the invaders. They know that their only real enemies in Eagle Valley are men with guns—the biggest hunters of all, creatures who can kill from a distance.

Lord and Lady Eagle continue to cry and dive at the trespassers. The two intruders pause briefly to observe the great eagles and then continue paddling their canoe downriver. Tally watches them disappear around a bend.

Soon his parents return to the nest. Still restless and upset, Lord Eagle lands on a branch above the nest to watch over his son.

New Wardrobe

June comes to Eagle Valley. Tally now spends more time moving about the big nest, and he is even starting to feed himself. This happens sometimes when his parents just leave food at the nest without ripping off pieces to give him. While pinning the food down with his feet, Tally uses his beak to tear off little chunks to eat.

At first his movements are clumsy and awkward. But this is how he must learn.

Lord and Lady Eagle are careful to keep the nest free of old bones and skin. Sometimes these leftovers are dropped to the ground below the nest, but usually they are carried farther away.

Throughout the nesting season the parents continue to bring fresh plants to the nest. These may be aspen leaves, marsh grass, or pine boughs. They give the nest a fresh and orderly look.

Occasionally both Tally and his parents eat plant material. Later they cough up some of this plant food and cast it off as small round balls of grass.

Tally keeps most of his second coat of fuzzy down. But about a month after hatching, his regular grownup feathers begin to appear. These are called "contour feathers."

Like human hair and nails, feathers are outgrowths from the skin. In many places on Tally's skin, small pimple-like bumps begin to grow. These bumps soon grow into slender columns of skin. As each column pushes upward, a central shaft takes form. From it, many little branches grow out. Each feather develops several hundred of these branches, which are called "barbs."

The barbs branch out from the main shaft. On each barb appear numerous smaller branches. These smaller branches have tiny hooks on them, which attach to the hooks of neighboring barbs. This hooking system helps hold the feathers together. Counting barbs, smaller branches, and hooks, one of Tally's large feathers may develop several million little branchings.

A feather is both soft and strong. If bent, it quickly pops back into shape. Because its central shaft is hollow, it is very lightweight.

Many of Tally's bones are hollow, too. A bird's skeleton is extremely strong and yet very light. When Tally is full grown, his entire bone skeleton will weigh only half as much as his coat of thousands of feathers.

The large contour feathers which appear on Tally's wings and tail are called "flight feathers." When each contour feather first grows out, it is enclosed in a slender case which looks like a light-blue straw. After a short time the case breaks apart. The feather unfolds and spreads its many branches.

As time passes, many contour feathers appear on Tally's growing body. Some are quite long. Others are just peeking through the fuzzy dark-grey down. This gives Tally a ragged appearance. He now begins to spend some time caring for his coat. He plucks out scraggly pieces of wooly down, which float away from the nest like pieces of grey cotton. He combs the new feathers with his beak. When Tally's body gets his complete grownup coat, there will still be a soft layer of down next to his skin.

Tally will need his new feathers when he begins to fly. The lightweight flight feathers have broad flat surfaces. When Tally flaps his wings, these flat surfaces will push against the air. This will lift the young eagle and move him forward through the air. The flight feathers are also necessary for gliding, turning, and slowing down.

His feathers will also serve him in other important ways. When the sun is hot, his feathers will act as a cooling system. They will shade his skin and protect it from heat. He can adjust his feathers so the air passes through to cool his skin.

When the weather turns cold, Tally's feathers will keep him warm.

Like other birds, an eagle has an extra membrane which slides over the eye from the side. It cleans and moistens the eye without completely blocking the light.

He will again adjust his feathers so they will hold a layer of warm air close to his body. The down and the contour feathers make a blanket which will keep him snug in freezing weather.

When it rains, Tally's undercoat of down and skin will stay dry. Water runs off the contour feathers because they overlap like shingles on a roof. Tally will also learn how to keep his feathers waterproof with preening oil, as he often sees his parents doing. Lord and Lady Eagle spend long periods each day caring for their feathers.

One day Tally watches Lord Eagle using his beak as a comb to straighten and clean each feather. From time to time Lord Eagle reaches back with his beak to the preening gland near his tail.

There he picks up a little preening oil and carefully combs it into his feathers.

Occasionally Lord Eagle moves his wings, fluffs his feathers, and shakes himself. Then he goes back to the business of preening.

It takes weeks for Tally's growing body to produce the many intricate contour feathers. From the time they first begin to appear, over a month passes before Tally acquires a full coat. When it is finally complete, he will have more than seven thousand of these beautiful feathers. Most of them are dark brown. But some are partly cream-colored. So Tally has a somewhat spotted appearance.

Four or five years will go by before Tally acquires the look of a mature Bald Eagle. He may be ten years old before his head and tail are completely white.

Feathers receive a lot of wear and tear. Some even get broken. Tally will grow a new coat of feathers every year. Each feather will be replaced by a new one. This molting happens slowly over many weeks so that Tally will have plenty of feathers at any one time. If he lost them all at once, his body would be unprotected and he could not fly.

First Flight

As Tally becomes larger and
stronger he also becomes more active.
Often now he hops around the nest.
At times he pounces on sticks or bones
as if they were make-believe prey. He
bites at pieces of tree bark and passing
insects. As with human children, this
play helps develop Tally's coordination.
The exercise strengthens his growing
muscles.

Tally extends his wings and tries flapping. At first these activities are clumsy and tiring. The new flight feathers make his wings heavy and awkward. Sometimes his wings get so tired that he doesn't even bother pulling them back to his side. They just droop lazily in the nest.

By the time eleven weeks have passed since hatching, Tally's movements are quicker and stronger. His wing flapping is steadier.

His wings now have all the flight feathers needed for lifting power. Sometimes when Tally flaps, he rises a short distance above the nest. This seems to startle him and he quickly drops back to the wide familiar platform.

One morning in July, Tally sees his father returning from upriver with a large fish. The young eagle is hungry and he starts to chirp. But Lord Eagle does not come to the nest. Instead he passes the nest and flies to his favorite perch. There he tears at the fish and eats it himself.

Tally continues his chirpy cries. Lord Eagle finishes eating the fish, cleans his beak, and then begins to preen his feathers. Tally moves restlessly about the nest. No more food is brought in that day.

Early next morning Tally looks for his parents to return with some breakfast for him. Finally Lady Eagle flies back with a fish. However, she does not deliver it to Tally. With the fish in her talons, Lady Eagle circles the nest tree and utters short cries. Tally hops about and chirps at her. After a few minutes of flying around the nest, she retires to a nearby perch and eats the fish herself.

Tally's hunger grows. Until now he has always had several meals a day. Now it has been almost two days since he has eaten anything.

Tally does not understand his parents' strange behavior. Lord and Lady Eagle are now trying to lure him from the nest with food. It is past mid-July and half the summer has gone in Eagle Valley. Tally has many things to learn before summer draws to a close and winter returns.

It is time for him to try to fly on his own. If Tally's parents continued to bring him easy meals, he might remain lazily in the nest the rest of the summer without ever leaving it.

Late in the afternoon Lord Eagle returns with another fish. He too flies around and around the nest. The fresh fish dangles from his talons. He passes close to the nest and cries to his son.

Tally hops to the edge of the nest. He chirps to his father and leans far out, trying to reach the fish.

Suddenly Tally is no longer in the nest. He has leaned too far forward and has slipped. He quickly opens his great wings—and finds himself gliding. He passes his mother's perch and several more trees. He slowly loses altitude, and the ground rushes by beneath him.

The edge of the river draws closer and closer. Tally doesn't know how to change direction in flight. Suddenly he finds himself over the river and only a few feet above the water. Frightened, he flaps his wings. His body begins to lift —but it is too late.

He crashes into the cold, unfamiliar water and topples forward. The strong current sweeps him beneath the surface. Over and over he rolls in the water.

The river carries Tally for several hundred feet. Then it sweeps him into a place where the current is slower. He comes to the surface and gasps for air. His parents circle and cry overhead.

Tally is weak and tired. Slowly he tries to flap his soggy wings. His soaked body is too heavy to fly. But the awkward flapping keeps him afloat and moving toward the shore of a nearby island.

Soon his feet touch the shallow bottom. The exhausted young eagle slowly wades ashore. With great effort he shakes his wet feathers and opens his wings to dry. Then he settles down on his stomach to rest.

After a couple of hours he rises and hops up on a stump. The warm sun has dried most of his feathers and he begins to preen them.

Soon Lord Eagle brings Tally a fresh fish. The young eagle quickly tears it apart and gulps it down in large chunks.

Evening comes. Tally sits and listens to the sounds of the moving river. Then he falls asleep. Close by, Lord and Lady Eagle sit perched in a tree. All night long they watch over Tally and guard him.

The Young Hunter

The next day Tally learns how
to become airborne. By running along
the shore and flapping his wings, he
can gradually rise into the air. At first his
flights are awkward and cover only short
distances.

Tally gradually learns that he must
get the movements of his wings working
together with the position of his tail.
In order to make turns, to rise and then
drop again, he must adjust the angle
of his tail like a rudder. At the same time
he must adjust his wings.

Tally's feathers also help him in braking. When landing, he turns his body up and extends his legs forward. He points his tail down and turns the wing surfaces up and slightly forward. The broad surfaces of his feathers push against the air. All this quickly slows him down.

As days pass, Tally's flights become longer. His flying improves with practice. The large chest muscles which drive his wings become stronger.

He follows his parents to places where columns of warm air rise from the earth. The rising air currents push upward on the flat feathers of his long broad wings and wide fan-shaped tail. Hardly flapping their wings at all, Tally and his parents rise with the air columns and soar in large circles.

From these great heights the eagles can see the lands stretching throughout Eagle Valley. Hawks and eagles seem to have the finest eyesight of any animals in the world. They can probably spot a fish from more than a mile away.

When he is not flying, Tally usually spends his time at the nest. It is safe here and a good place to rest. While he is learning the art of hunting, his parents continue to bring him food here. The

nest still makes the best dinner table
for the eagle family.

Tally's hunting lessons begin as he
follows his parents on trips away from
the nest area. His first experiences are
with fishing. He follows his mother
to one of her favorite fishing spots on
Wild River. They sit perched in a tall
tree above a side channel of the main
river. They wait for a fish to stray into
the shallow water.

The first time Lady Eagle drops
from the tree with a long swoop to snatch
a fish from the moving water, Tally
follows right behind her. He is so close
that when she suddenly slows down in
order to strike beneath the water, he
almost bumps into her. A collision would
knock them both into the river.

Whenever his mother catches a fish,
Tally quickly flies to her side. He
crowds against her and snatches pieces
of the kill. It seems that Tally is always
ready to eat. Now that he is more active,
his body needs more energy.

Tally also tries to fish, but at first
he isn't very successful. He notices a
Great Blue Heron slowly wading on long
legs through quiet pools, searching for
a fish or a frog. The heron's long neck
strikes out quickly as he stabs his prey
with his dagger-shaped bill.

Now Tally attempts to catch fish by wading in from the shore. The cold, deep water and the wary, quick-moving fish soon teach him this is not the best method. Wading may work fine for a bird with long legs and a long bill, but it doesn't work for an eagle.

Tally tries swooping down from a perch like his mother. But he finds it hard to control his quick descent and to know exactly when to check his speed and strike beneath the surface. To make things worse, the fish are often hard to see in the moving water and they disappear quickly. Tally works very hard, but he has many failures for the few fish he actually catches.

In addition to fishing, Tally learns to find food in the marshes along Wild River. His parents teach him to fly low over these areas. He looks for small mammals and birds, such as Muskrats or ducks, which have strayed from the protection of hidden channels, thick bushes, and tall reeds.

Each day Tally learns something new about hunting. He begins to know the best times and the best places to look for food. He also learns what kinds of animals to chase, and what methods are best in hunting each kind.

In time Tally will become an excellent fisherman. He will also be able to catch prey in the sky. He will develop the speed and turning ability to snatch fast-flying birds right out of the air.

Besides taking prey from the water and the air, Tally will also be skillful at hunting prey on the land. Sometimes he will hunt in the mountains or out on the vast prairies, where he will catch rabbits or ground squirrels. Because the Bald Eagle can catch so many kinds of prey, so many different ways, he is one of the world's most exciting hunting birds.

Tally will also have the strength and speed to hunt and kill larger animals such as Coyotes or Pronghorn Antelope. But smaller animals are easier and safer to hunt. So he will rarely bother the larger ones.

One clear August day Tally is resting at the nest. He notices his father soaring high above Wild River. Tally flies out to where he can find the rising air currents. He soars to a good height, then closes his wings a little and makes a short dive. He drops with great speed and then swoops upward once again. As if he is playing, he repeats with another short dive, climbs, and then drops again.

Soon Tally opens his wings and rises higher and higher toward his father. He joins Lord Eagle high above Wild River. When the two fly close together, Tally looks a little larger than his father. Actually their bodies are the same size. But Tally's wing feathers and tail feathers are slightly longer. These feathers give him extra flight surface during these early times of learning. Later when he molts and grows a new set of feathers, they will be the same length as his father's.

Tally makes another short dive while Lord Eagle continues his glide

OSPREY

upward. Some distance downriver Tally
sees an Osprey. The other bird soars
slowly over the moving water. He is
hunting for fish, his only food.

Tally sees the Osprey close his wings
and drop almost straight down toward
the river. Unlike the eagles, he plunges
his whole body beneath the surface.
An instant later the Osprey rises, grasping
a trout. With the fish in his claws, the
Osprey heads upriver. He approaches the
area where Tally and his father are
soaring far above.

Tally hears the swish of rushing
air. He turns to see his father make
a rapid dive toward the Osprey. Lord
Eagle screams as he closes in. The Osprey
cries out and makes a quick turn to
escape. But Lord Eagle also makes a sharp
turn and continues the chase.

Suddenly Lord Eagle sweeps beneath the Osprey. In midair he turns over on his back and thrusts his talons at the other bird. The Osprey cries again, releases the trout, and flies upriver. The fish tumbles toward the surface. Lord Eagle banks and follows the falling fish. He snatches the fish from the water as it hits the surface. The Osprey calls out again but continues flying upriver.

The Bald Eagles do not often bother the Ospreys. Today, however, the Osprey has been fishing near the eagles' nest. Perhaps this was Lord Eagle's way of reminding the trespasser that the sky above this stretch of Wild River belongs to the eagle family.

Wild hunters like Tally and his parents play an important role in nature. There are many kinds of animals which can reproduce very quickly. Sparrows, mice, rabbits, and deer, for example, multiply rapidly. If the number of these animals increase too much, there will not be enough food for all to eat. When this happens, many animals die of starvation.

Wild hunters like wolves, Coyotes, hawks, and eagles help to keep these numbers at proper levels. Often they

hunt weak and sick animals, leaving
the strong and healthy ones to raise new
families.

The hunters themselves may
become prey to other hunters. Little
insects are hunted by large insects.
Large insects are hunted by small birds.
Small birds are hunted by large birds.
All these relations of hunter and prey are
important in the complicated and
delicate ways of nature.

Farewell to Summer

The weeks of summer have passed, and October has come to Eagle Valley. The leaves of the Cottonwood and Aspen trees have taken on new colors of red, yellow, gold, and brown.

Almost three months have passed since Tally took his first flight from the nest. Since then he has grown greatly in strength and knowledge. The daily hunting trips with his parents have taught him much about the world in which he lives. There are still many things to learn, but Tally will have to learn these on his own—in the months and years ahead.

Even now he is spending less and less time with his parents. Often he roams up and down the river's path by himself.

The fall season seems to have brought with it a sense of excitement. Tally sees animals busy throughout Eagle Valley. Squirrels are scampering along the forest floor gathering pine cones to store for the coming winter. The Beavers are spending long hours cutting fresh branches and willows to float back to the pond and store on the muddy bottom. These will provide the Beavers with a winter food supply through the long frozen months.

The Moose moves noisily about in his willow patch. He thrashes the willows and small trees with his huge antlers, which are now full grown. The Moose is rubbing the old skin from the antlers. This skin is called "velvet." The loose pieces of velvet hang like dark ribbons from his white antlers.

Families of ducks and other birds are now banding together and roaming the river bottoms in large flocks. Soon most of these flocks will leave Eagle Valley and wing their way south.

One of Tally's favorite activities is chasing Coots. These black duck-like birds have now banded together in flocks to feed on the river. When Tally makes a passing dive over a group of them, the frightened birds dive beneath the surface. When they finally come up, Tally sweeps low over them again. If he is hunting seriously, Tally repcats this several times until one of them becomes too tired to make quick dives. This is the one Tally will catch for a meal.

At other times when Tally dives, the Coots will attempt to take off from the water. They run along the surface flapping their wings in order to pick up enough speed for flight. Sometimes one will fall behind the others or wander from the main flock. Again, if Tally is hungry, this is usually the one he will try to capture.

Sometimes Tally will chase Coots and other animals without really trying to catch them. But Tally never kills animals just for fun. He kills only when he is hungry.

The weather turns colder. The colorful leaves begin to slip from the trees and float to the ground.

One cold morning Tally heads out to catch his breakfast. He notices a plump fish swimming in shallow water. Tally quickly banks and dives. With outstretched feet, he aims for his target. Suddenly he hits a thin, hard film on the water's surface. The clear film cracks and breaks. But Tally is so startled that he forgets the fish and lands on the nearby bank.

Carefully he puts a foot back out on the surface. It crunches. Tally hops back and looks at the unfamiliar ice.

Tally becomes aware that more and more birds are moving south. Long V-shaped flocks of Canadian Geese pass high overhead. Ducks and other birds also pass over—all heading south. This movement of the birds seems to make Tally restless.

One day the air turns still and quiet. Low gray clouds cover the entire valley and block out the surrounding mountain peaks.

Tally is perched downriver from the nest. Soon a cold breeze begins to come out of the north. A soft white speck floats down and hits Tally's beak. It

quickly disappears, leaving a small drop
of water. Tally shakes his beak and
wipes off the drop on the branch.

Soon many of the white flakes are
falling around him, settling on his
head. Again Tally shakes and fluffs his
feathers. But finally he accepts the falling
snow and sits quietly. On his perch
Tally sleeps warmly in his clothing of
fuzzy down and contour feathers. The
next morning he awakens to find Eagle
Valley a world of whiteness. Except for
the moving waters of the river, everything
is covered with a blanket of new snow.

Tally looks down at the white strip
of snow piled on his perch. He steps
sideways, sliding his feet against the light
snow. White puffs fall from his perch
and drift to the ground.

The day is sunny but cold and very
quiet. There are no other animals
around, not even Tally's parents. They
have spent the night farther upriver.

Without warning, Tally takes off
to follow the many birds which have
already departed to the south.

He leaves his perch, turns, and heads
downriver. He is beginning a journey
which will lead him far beyond Eagle
Valley. There are no preparations, no
delays, no good-bys. He just leaves.

Some young eagles stay with their parents for their first winter. Others leave after the nesting season is completed. Young Bald Eagles have been known to fly alone through unfamiliar land for over a thousand miles in just a few days.

Heading south, Tally continues to fly along the path of Wild River. Stands of Cottonwood trees and white hills glide beneath him. His strong wings carry him toward the end of Eagle Valley, and soon he enters a deep canyon. The snow-covered mountains rise on both sides.

ADULT BALD EAGLE

Tally flies around a bend in the
river. Suddenly he sees a young Coyote
feeding on the top of a large dead animal.
The dead animal is an old Elk which
probably drowned while trying to cross
the swift water. Its body has washed
up on a small gravel bar in the middle of
the river.

Most of the time Bald Eagles prefer
to hunt and catch their own fresh food.
But, like many hunters, the eagle finds
it hard to pass up an easy meal—especially
in winter when food is difficult to find.

Tally lands in a tree and watches
the Coyote feed on the Elk. The young
eagle has not eaten for some time, and
his long flight has made him hungry.
He waits for only a few minutes and then
swoops down toward the feeding Coyote.

Tally screams as he approaches.

The startled Coyote looks up. Tally
cries again and swoops closely over him.
Then Tally turns and sweeps in again.

This time he clips the frightened Coyote
on the rump with his sharp talons.
The Coyote lets out a yelp, plunges into
the river, and swims toward the bank.
He seems to realize that he is no match
for the large eagle.

Tally is not interested in fighting
either—only in eating. He lands on the
Elk carcass and begins to feed.

It is late in the afternoon when
Tally finishes feeding. He leaves the Elk
and flies to a perch high above the river.
Soon darkness comes.

Tally rests well through the night.
The next morning he leaves his perch
and heads downriver. His broad wings
move him strongly and swiftly.

Soon he passes out of the canyon.
On and on down Wild River he continues. Behind him the mountains
surrounding Eagle Valley appear smaller
and smaller. Ahead await new lands,
new experiences, and new dangers.

Beyond Eagle Valley

Will Tally survive this winter and other years to come? There is no way for us to know. We can only hope that Tally will live a long and healthy life. Hopefully, he will find a mate and return in three or four years to these high Teton Mountains of Wyoming to raise families of his own.

Beyond Eagle Valley he will find new lands and new sights. He will fly over places where his ancestors have flown for thousands and thousands of years. But now the land has changed greatly.

Today most of the wild regions have
disappeared. Instead, Tally will find
farms, ranches, towns, and smoking
factories. He will pass over highways busy
with moving automobiles. Large metal
airplanes will roar by in the noisy
skyways. Wherever Tally flies, he will
meet man and his civilization.

During his first winter he will live
mostly alone. He will rarely see other
young Bald Eagles. For eagle parents are
now raising fewer and fewer young
eagles each year.

Our national bird once lived in
great numbers in every state of the Union
except Hawaii. Now fewer than ten
states have more than a dozen active
Bald Eagle nests. In the lower 48 states
there are probably less than 700 breeding
pairs of Bald Eagles. No one knows
how many remain in Alaska, but even
there the numbers seem to be declining.

Our national bird is disappearing
because throughout our history we have
not treated him very well. After declaring
him our national symbol, we waited
for 158 years before we protected him
under the law. This law, passed in 1940,
makes it illegal to kill or harm the Bald
Eagles. By 1940, however, much of
the population of the white-headed birds

had already been killed by man and his civilization.

Even after the law was passed, men continued to kill Bald Eagles in the Territory of Alaska before it became a state. The law protecting Bald Eagles did not apply to the Territory because some Alaskans in the fur and fish industries did not want it. They thought the eagles were hurting their business. So the industries got special permission from the government in Washington to keep on killing Bald Eagles.

The government in Alaska even paid people to kill the Bald Eagles. A reward of one or two dollars was paid for each dead bird brought to Alaska officials. In a few years rewards were paid for over 100,000 Bald Eagles. Probably another 100,000 were killed in Alaska by people who didn't collect the money.

Soon after the great slaughter, scientists found out that killing Bald Eagles had been a serious mistake. Slaughtering them did not help the fur or fish industries at all. The eagles had been wrongly blamed.

Today the Bald Eagle has complete protection throughout the United States —including the state of Alaska. Heavy fines and penalties can be given to people

who kill or injure our national bird.
It is against the law to disturb the nests
or eggs of Bald Eagles. It is even illegal
to own parts of their bodies, such as
feathers. But there are still some people
who break the law and shoot the great
birds.

Young Bald Eagles look so much
like Golden Eagles that many of them
are illegally shot or poisoned each year
by stockmen, especially sheepherders.
Eagles are wrongly blamed for killing a
large number of lambs on the open ranges
each year. These few irresponsible
ranchers seem to forget that the eagles
help them by controlling rabbits and
rodents—animals that compete with the
sheep for the grass on the range.

In any case, laws are not enough
to protect our national birds. As our
civilization has marched across America,
it has destroyed most of the wild natural
areas. The Bald Eagle needs undisturbed
areas in which to live. His home must
have tall forests, clear skies, fresh water,
and an abundance of wildlife.

With our machines, highways, and
buildings, we have ruined most of these
wild areas. We have polluted land, water,
and air with our waste and our noise.
By killing off other wild animals, this

pollution has also ruined much of the food supply for the Bald Eagles.

A special man-made danger to eagles comes from electric powerlines. Many eagles are found dead each year beneath power poles they used for perches. If an eagle touches the wrong wires, the electric shock kills him instantly.

Today the greatest danger to Bald Eagles comes from the poisons called "pesticides." These are the chemicals we have sprayed on gardens, farms, and forests to kill unwanted pests such as insects. The ones especially harmful to wildlife are the "hard" pesticides, which remain poisonous for a very long time. DDT is an example of a hard pesticide.

Recently scientists have learned that the hard pesticides are harmful to all living creatures. When pesticides are sprayed on crops to kill unwanted insects, they often kill helpful insects—and other kinds of animals as well.

Hard pesticides have spread all around the world. These poisons are now found in fish living in the middle of the oceans and in penguins living near the South Pole. These chemicals are now in the bodies of all living beings on earth—including people. Even Eskimos near the Arctic Circle, hundreds of miles

from the nearest farm, have traces of these chemicals in their bodies.

When the Bald Eagle eats fish, the chemicals from the fish build up in his body. Sometimes the poisons kill the great birds immediately. Sometimes the poisons attack their nervous systems, interfering with their flying and hunting.

Some pesticides also harm the ability of Bald Eagle parents to raise families. The chemicals pass from a mother eagle into the egg she lays. The poisons may kill the baby eagles before or after hatching.

The pesticides can even disturb the shell-making process within the mother's body. She may lay eggs with thin shells—or even no shells at all. If the shell is weak, the egg may not protect the baby eagle until it is time for him to hatch.

Today in America, young eagles like Tally are becoming fewer and fewer. The day may soon come when this magnificent wild creature will disappear from the face of the earth—lost forever. Once the Bald Eagles become extinct, there will be no way to bring them back to life.

As our national bird, the Bald Eagle represents many things—natural beauty, life, strength, courage, loyalty, and freedom. These are qualities which beckoned our forefathers to this great land and they have been an important part of our heritage.

Yet the day may soon come when the only Bald Eagles we see will be lifeless images on coins, seals, and advertisements. If the Bald Eagle becomes extinct, it will mean our country has lost more than a beautiful bird. It will mean that we have let our land be changed too much by our machines, buildings, highways, waste, and noise. The decline of our national bird should be a warning that we have treated our land foolishly.

Perhaps we still have a chance to save some of our Bald Eagles and other beautiful wild creatures. To do so, we must learn to have more respect for other living creatures. Rather than push them aside because of our own selfish wishes, we human beings must learn to share the earth with them.

Also, we must protect and extend our few remaining wilderness areas. We must stop the foolish use of deadly chemicals which bring harm to all living things. We must stop needless practices which pollute the land, the water, and the air with our careless wastes.

If the time comes when our beautiful national bird no longer flies the sky of this land, it will be a tragedy for Americans, and for all the world.

Let us try harder and hope that there will always be Bald Eagles—wild and free—for future generations of Americans to admire and enjoy.

NOTE ABOUT ANIMAL NAMES

When scientists write about animals, they often use capital letters for the names of species. A species is a group of animals so closely related that they can mate and produce young in the wild. Examples in this book: Bald Eagle, Golden Eagle, Coot, Muskrat, Elk.

For larger groups and families of animals, less closely related, scientists generally do not use capital letters. Examples in this book: eagles, hawks, ducks, rabbits, deer.

Index

ABOUT THE AUTHOR

John F. Turner has spent thousands of hours studying and photographing birds and other wild animals near his birthplace (Jackson Hole) in Wyoming's Teton Mountains. With his wife and child he lives near Moose, Wyoming.

Recently he took office as one of the youngest members of the Wyoming House of Representatives, where he was chosen as the outstanding freshman representative.

Holding a master's degree in zoology, he is studying for a doctorate in wildlife ecology. He was one of the founders of the nation's first ENACT (Environment Action Organization) and has been a member of the U.S. Interior Department's SCOPE (Student Council on Pollution and Environment).

"The photographs in this book," says Mr. Turner, "are the result of time and perseverance over a number of years. Many of them were taken a hundred feet up while dangling in a swaying tree, one arm hanging on for survival and the other shooting a telephoto lens." The photograph on the next page shows the "blind" he built high in a tree in order to photograph Bald Eagles in their nest.